Musolympics Song Book

Frances Turnbull

Copyright © 2018 Frances Turnbull

Musolympics Song Book
All rights reserved
Musicaliti Publishing, Bolton, UK

ISBN: 978-1907935862

www.musicaliti.co.uk

Contents

Ukulele Tuning and Chords	5
Swimming	7
Cycling	13
Athletics	19
Rowing	25
Gymnastics	31
Tennis	37
Session pictures	43
Write your own song	45

Musical Munchies Song Book

Ukulele Chords

Ukuleles are small, accessible and relatively cheap instruments that can be used to play the accompaniment to many songs.

Each string should be tuned to specific notes (can be found on tuned instruments like xylophones, pianos or recorders etc.). The standard ukulele tuning is:

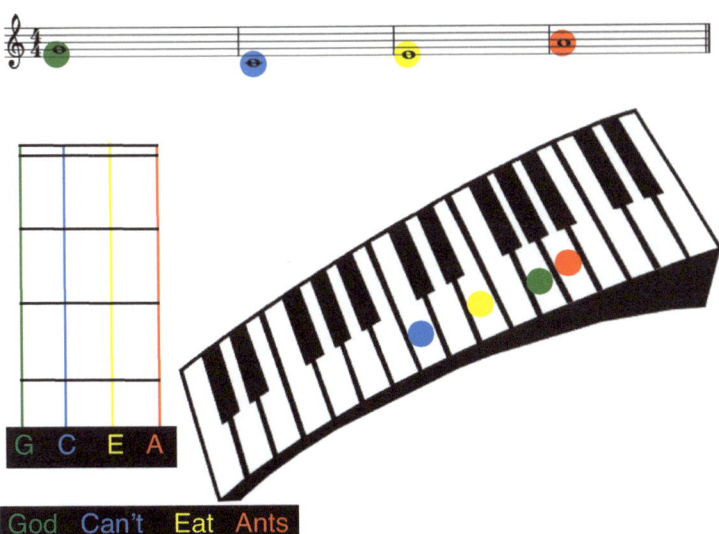

God Can't Eat Ants

By placing your fingers on the frets at the positions on the pictures, (between the lines), you change the sound of the strings into chords when strummed altogether.

musicaliti

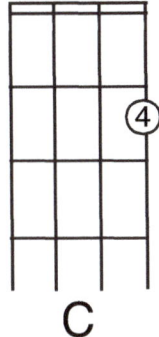
C

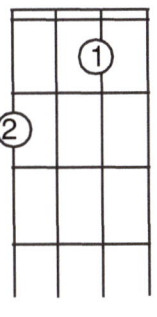
F

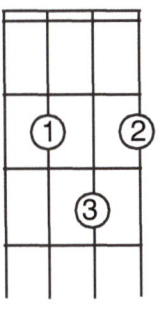
G

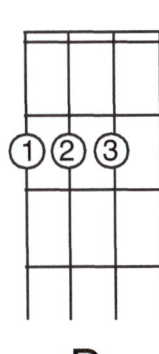
D

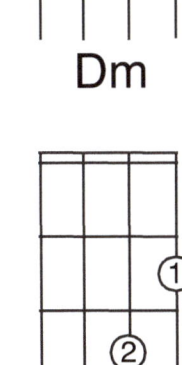
Am

Dm

Em

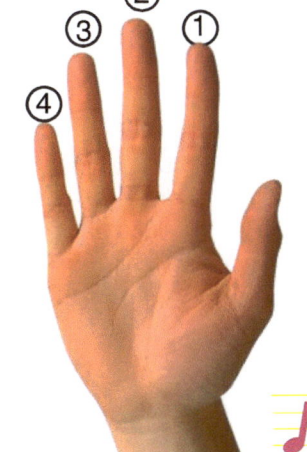

musicaliti

ABOUT THE BOOK

This book is about British Olympic champions: 2008-2012-2016

Swimming

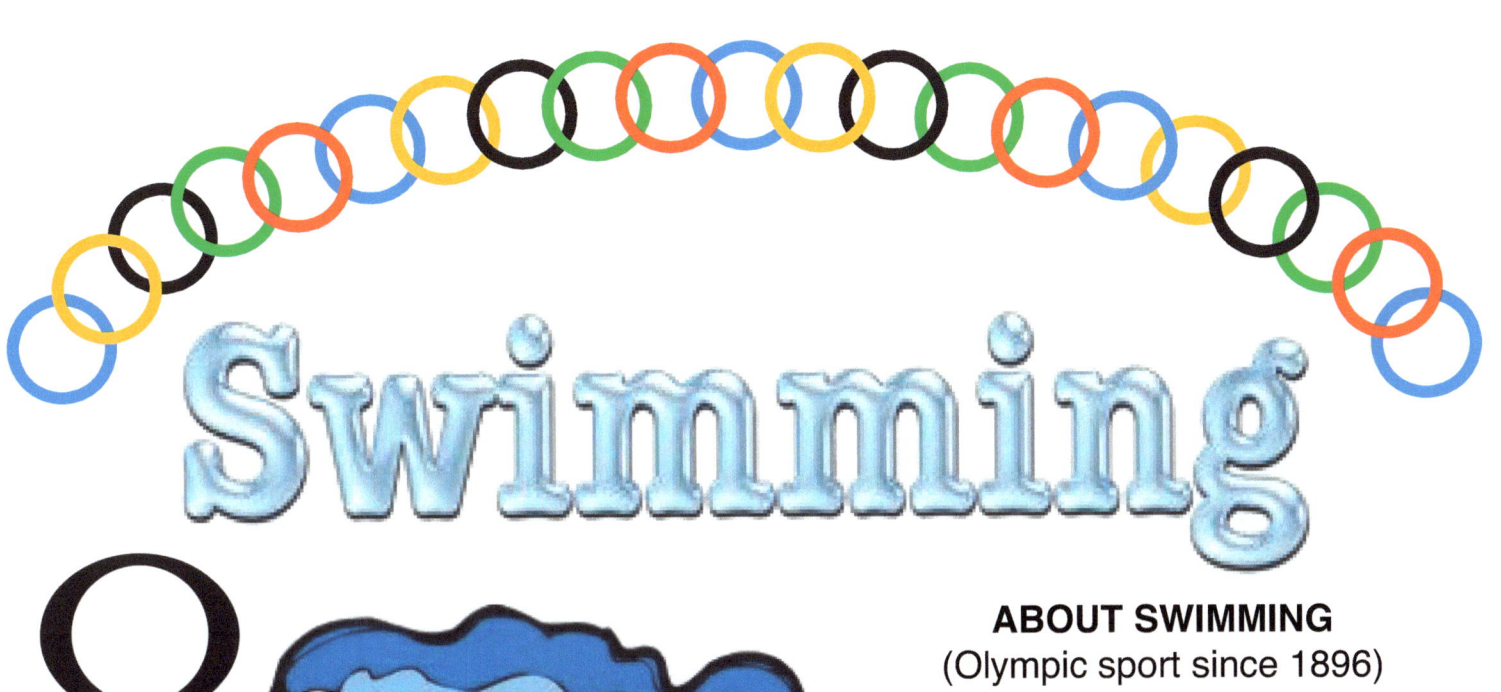

ABOUT SWIMMING
(Olympic sport since 1896)

Swimming competitions used to be held in rivers, lakes and even the icy Mediterranean Ocean, where swimmers were sailed out by boat and had to swim back to the shore. Swimming pools have changed a lot and are now temperature-controlled and are even designed to reduce waves.

ABOUT COMPETITION
Women have been allowed to compete since 1912 and both men and women can now take part in 16 events using 4 different strokes. Freestyle distances can be 50-1500 metres with only 8 swimmers.

2 GOLD medals 2008

2 BRONZE medals 2012

SWIMMING

Women's 400m freestyle Women's 800m freestyle

REBECCA ADLINGTON

17 February 1989

SILVER medal 2016

SWIMMING

Women's 200 metres

SIOBHAN-MARIE O-CONNOR

29 November 1995

PHOTO CREDIT:
Picture by Richard Gillin from St Albans, UK - Becky AdlingtonUploaded by Kafuffle, CC BY-SA 2.0, https://commons.wikimedia.org/w/index.php?curid=21377206

PHOTO CREDIT:
Picture by Oleg Bkhambri (Voltmetro) - Own work, CC BY-SA 4.0, https://commons.wikimedia.org/w/index.php?curid=42060903

Rebecca Adlington OBE was born in Mansfield, Nottinghamshire and is a British freestyle swimmer.

She won two gold medals in the 2008 Beijing Summer Olympics and broke the record for 800m, which was set in 1988 by Janet Evans, when Rebecca was only 6 months old. She is the first British Olympics swimming champion since 1988 and the first British swimmer to win 2 medals at one Olympic Games since 1908 and Britain's most successful swimmer in 100 years.

She started swimming when she was 4 years old and began taking part in competitions when she was 10 years old. She always buys a new swimming costumer for every big competition. She was given the title OBE (Order of the British Empire at the 2009 New Years Honours list.

SWIMMING GOLD
Beijing Olympics, 2008

SWIMMING BRONZE
London Olympics, 2012

Rebecca Adlington OBE was born in Mansfield, Nottinghamshire and is a retired freestyle swimmer.

She won two bronze medals in the 2012 Summer Olympics in London. She was the first British Olympics swimming champion since 1988 and the first British swimmer to win Olympic gold medals since 1908 (2008 Beijing Olympics).

She started swimming when she was 4 years old and began taking part in competitions when she was 10 years old. She always buys a new swimming costumer for every big competition.

Siobhan-Marie O'Connor was born in Bath, and is a specialist in the 200 metres individual medley.

She won medals at every level of competition in the 2016 Summer Olympics in Rio. She set a new record for Britain in the 200m Individual Medley of 2:06:88. She also holds the British records for the 100 metre breaststroke and the 4 x 100-metre mixed medley relay.

She used to do both gymnastics and swimming, but stopped gymnastics when she started swimming in competitions when she was 10 years old. Her hobby is shopping!

SWIMMING SILVER
Rio Olympics 2016

Musolympics Song Book

Bounce High

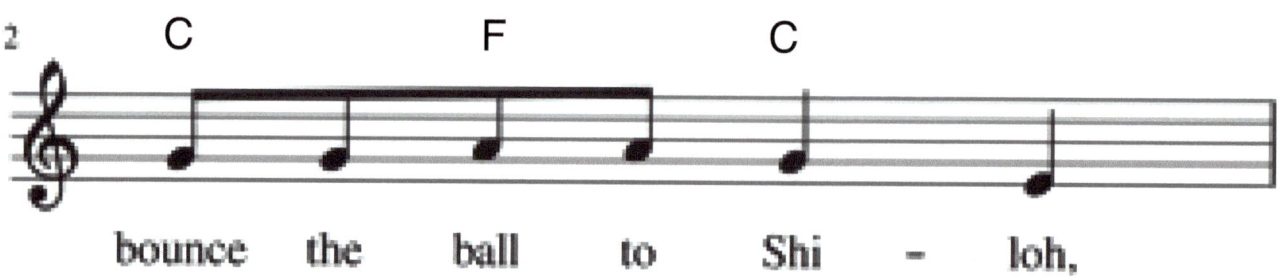

Bounce high, bounce low,

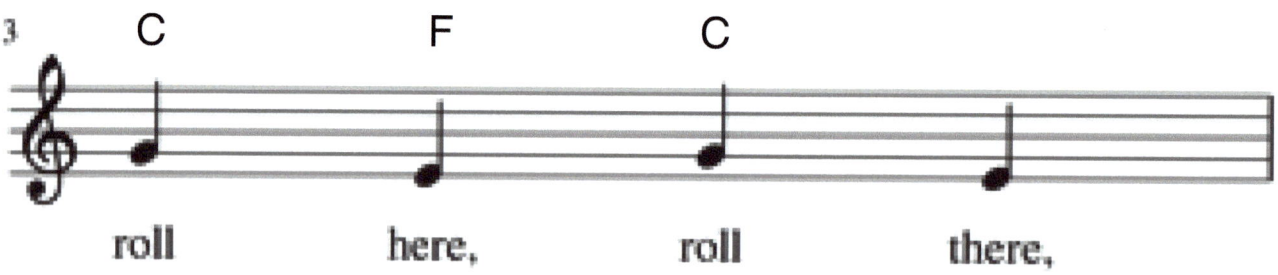

bounce the ball to Shi - loh,

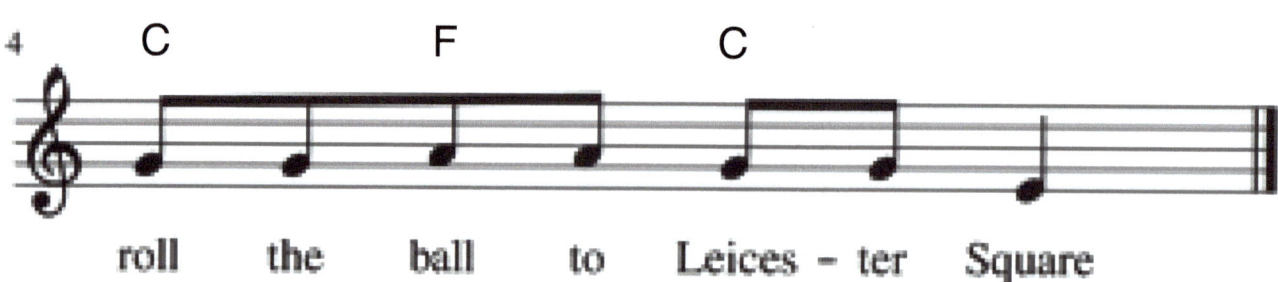

roll here, roll there,

roll the ball to Leices - ter Square

Frances Turnbull

Old Brass Wagon

Cir - cle to the left, old brass wa - gon,
Cir - cle to the right, old brass wa - gon,
Ev - 'ry - bo - dy down, old brass wa - gon,
Ev - 'ry - bo - dy in, old brass wa - gon,

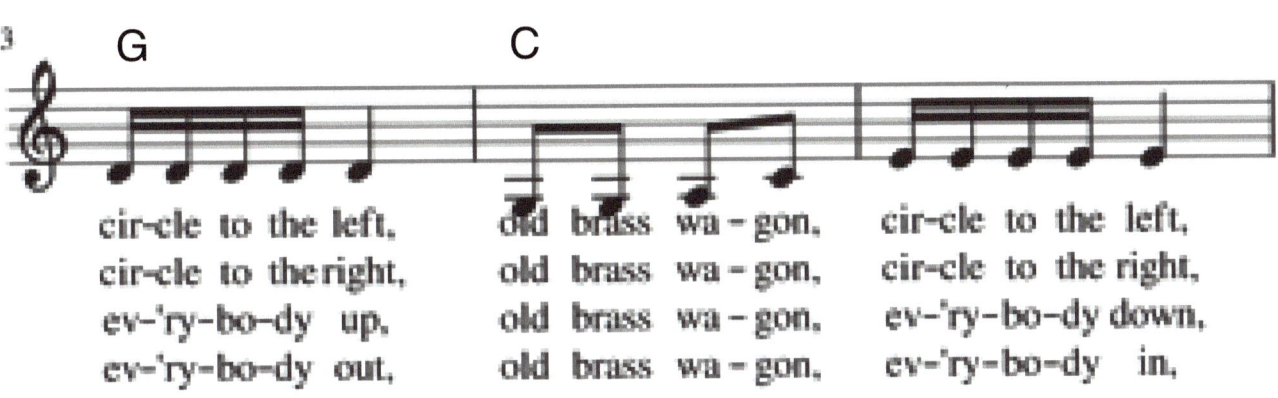

cir-cle to the left, old brass wa-gon, cir-cle to the left,
cir-cle to the right, old brass wa-gon, cir-cle to the right,
ev-'ry-bo-dy up, old brass wa-gon, ev-'ry-bo-dy down,
ev-'ry-bo-dy out, old brass wa-gon, ev-'ry-bo-dy in,

old brass wa - gon, you're the one my dar - ling!
old brass wa - gon, you're the one my dar - ling!
old brass wa - gon, you're the one my dar - ling!
old brass wa - gon, you're the one my dar - ling!

Musolympics Song Book

Cycling

ABOUT CYCLING
(Olympic sport since 1896)

Bicycles were invented in 1871 and they were called Penny Farthings because the front wheel was much larger (like a farthing) than the back one (like a penny). There are 4 types of cycling competitions: road, track, mountain biking and BMX.

ABOUT TRACK
Track cyclists ride around a track shaped like a funnel at 42 degrees. This is called a velodrome and makes the bikes go faster. Some competitions involve a team of two, taking turns to race, with a motor bike leading the riders, called the Olympic Sprint.

Musolympics Song Book

3 GOLD medals, 2008

2 GOLD medals, 2012

CYCLING

Men's Sprint, Men's Kierin, Men's team sprint

CHRIS HOY

23 March 1976

6 GOLD medals, 2016

CYCLING

TRACK CYCLIST

JASON KENNY

23 March 1988

PHOTO CREDIT:
Picture by Mark Harkin - 100_5810Uploaded by BaldBoris, CC BY 2.0, https://commons.wikimedia.org/w/index.php?curid=21367747

PHOTO CREDIT:
Picture by Jim Thurston - Flickr: Jason Kenny & Ed Clancy, CC BY-SA 2.0, https://commons.wikimedia.org/w/index.php?curid=25637239

Sir Chris Hoy MBE was born in Edinburgh and is a track cyclist representing England and Scotland. He has won many world championships and won 3 gold medals in the Beijing Olympics, making him the most successful Olympic male cyclist of all time. He is Scotland's most successful Olympian and the first Briton to win 3 gold medals in one Olympic games since 1908.

He was inspired to cycle by the film E.T. (Extra Terrestrial) and raced BMX's until he was 14 years old, also taking part in rowing and rugby at school. He was given the title MBE (Member of the British Empire) in 2005 and then the title of Knight Bachelor in the 2009 New Years Honours list.

CYCLING
GOLD
Beijing
Olympics, 2008

Sir Chris Hoy MBE was born in Edinburgh and is a track cyclist who represents England at the Olympics and and Scotland in the Commonwealth Games. He won eleven world championships and six Olympic championships. He won two gold medals in the 2012 London Olympics.

As a child, he was inspired to cycle after watching a film about an alien who rides a bike (E.T., Extra Terrestrial). He raced BMX's until he was 14 years old, as well as rowing and playing rugby.

CYCLING
GOLD
London
Olympics, 2012

Jason Kenny CBE was born in Farnworth, Bolton and is track cyclist who represented England at the 2016 Olympics. He won the team sprint, the individual sprint and the Keirin, totalling 6 gold medals. He won his first medal when he was 20 years old.

Jason's mum is a teacher and his dad is a structural engineer. His uncle took him to see a Velodrome in Manchester when he was younger, and he says his school PE teachers inspired him to win!

CYCLING
GOLD
Rio Olympics
2016

Snail snail

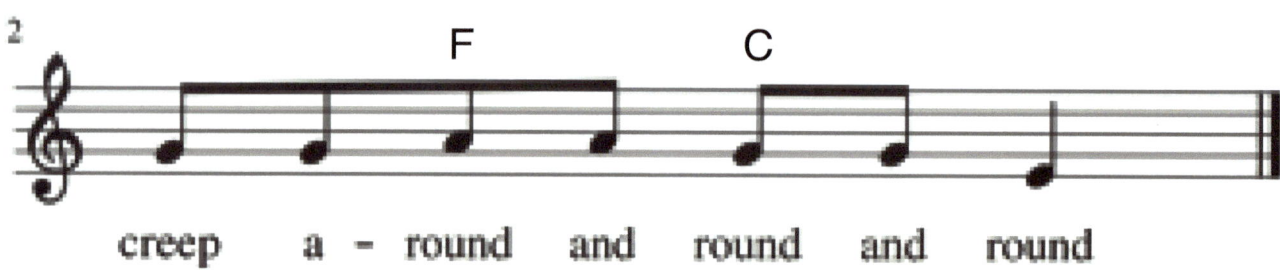

Frances Turnbull

How many miles

How ma-ny miles to Ba - by - lon? Three score and ten.

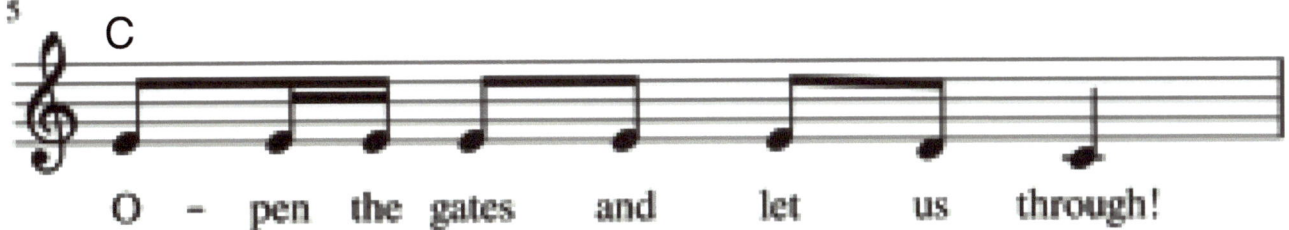

Will I get back be-fore you do? Yes and back a - gain

O - pen the gates and let us through!

Not with - out a beck and bow!

Here's the beck! Here's the bow, o-pen the gates and let us through!

ABOUT ATHLETICS
(the original Olympic sport)

Athletics was the first sport to be held at the Olympics since 776BC, as well as European fairs, including Ireland's Tailteann and Scotland's Highland Games.

Women were first included in the Olympics in 1928 and now compete in almost as many programmes as men.

Historically Americans were the top champions, challenged only by USSR and East Germany, but now many Caribbean countries are challenging them strongly, with African states dominating distance events.

GOLD medal 2008

SILVER medal 2012

ATHLETICS

Women 400 metres

CHRISTINE OHURUOGU

17 May 1984

2 GOLD medals 2016

ATHLETICS

Men's 5,000 metres
Men's 10,000 metres

MO FARAH

23 March 1983

PHOTO CREDIT:
By Flickr user Nick J Webb - Cropped version of Christina Ohuruogu on Flickr, CC BY 2.0, https://commons.wikimedia.org/w/index.php?curid=5016867

PHOTO CREDIT:
By U.S. Army - Silver medalist Spc. Paul Chelimo at Rio Olympic Games 5,000 meters medal ceremony photos by Tim Hipps, U.S. Army IMCOM Public Affairs, CC BY 2.0, https://commons.wikimedia.org/w/index.php?curid=50897910

Christine Ohuruogu MBE was born in Newham, East London and is an English sprinter, and was the Commonwealth, World and Olympic Champion for running 400 metres in 49.61 seconds. Her medal was the 50th gold medal for Britain and she is the first British woman champion of the 400 metre sprint.

She has 8 brothers and sisters, and one of her sisters is also a top sprinter in her age group. She received a degree from University College London in Linguistics in 2005, where she also played netball. She started competing professionally in athletics in 2004.

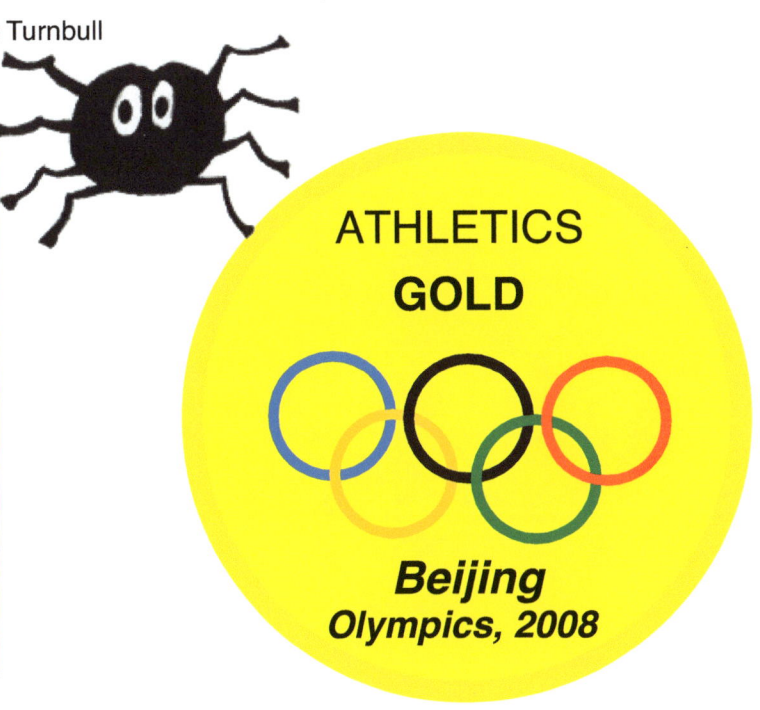

Christine Ohuruogu MBE was born in Newham, East London and is an English sprinter who specialises in the Women's 400 metres. She won the silver medal at the London Olympics in 2012. Her personal best time is 49.41 seconds.

Christine used to play netball and athletics at school, and she has a degree from University College London in languages (linguistics). She has eight brothers and sisters, and wrote children's books about children going to a special athlete-training school.

Sir Mo Farah CBE was born in Mogadishu, Somalia and is an English distance runner who specialises in distance doubles. He was the World Champion and former Olympic and Commonwealth Champion. He has the most medals out of all British athletes in history.

When he was little, Mo was a refugee because his country became too dangerous for him to stay. When he was 8 he moved to London to live with his dad. He loves cars and first wanted to be a mechanic or a football player, until his PE teacher encouraged him to develop his running skills. He also has a twin brother!

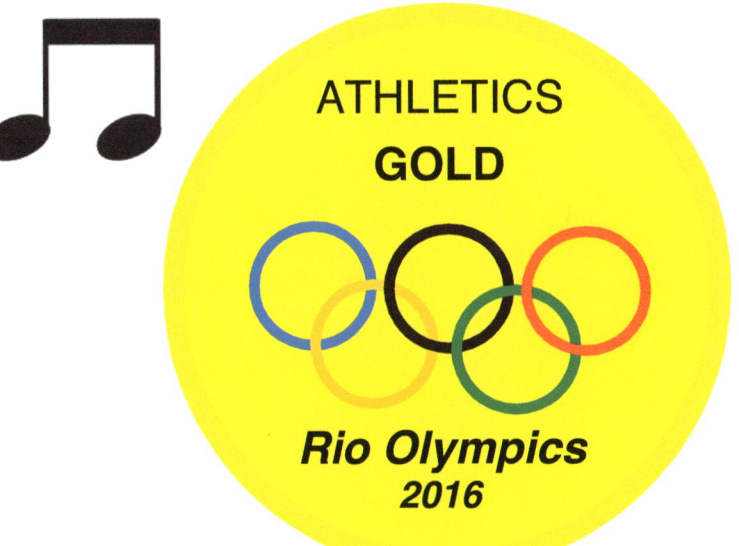

Down came my Friend

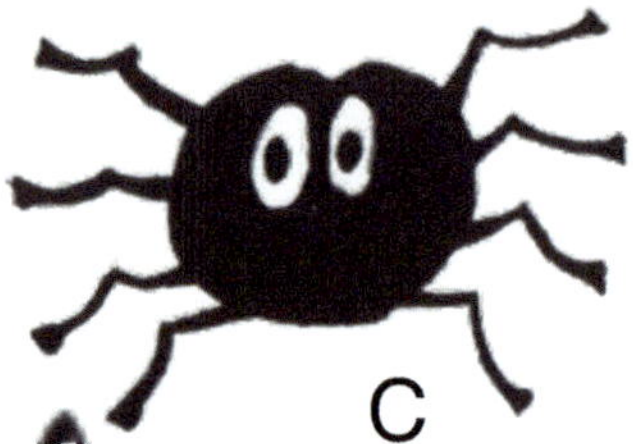

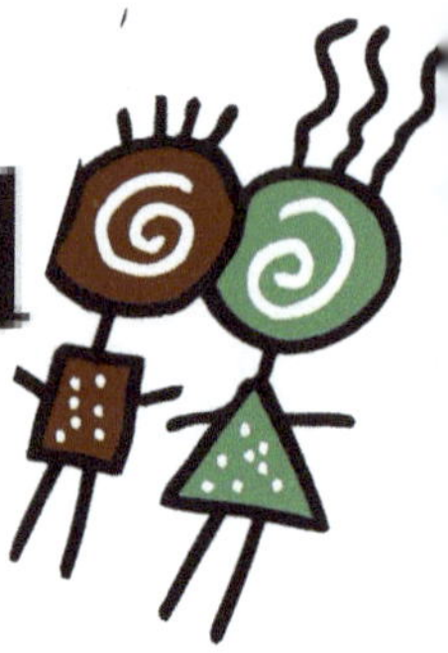

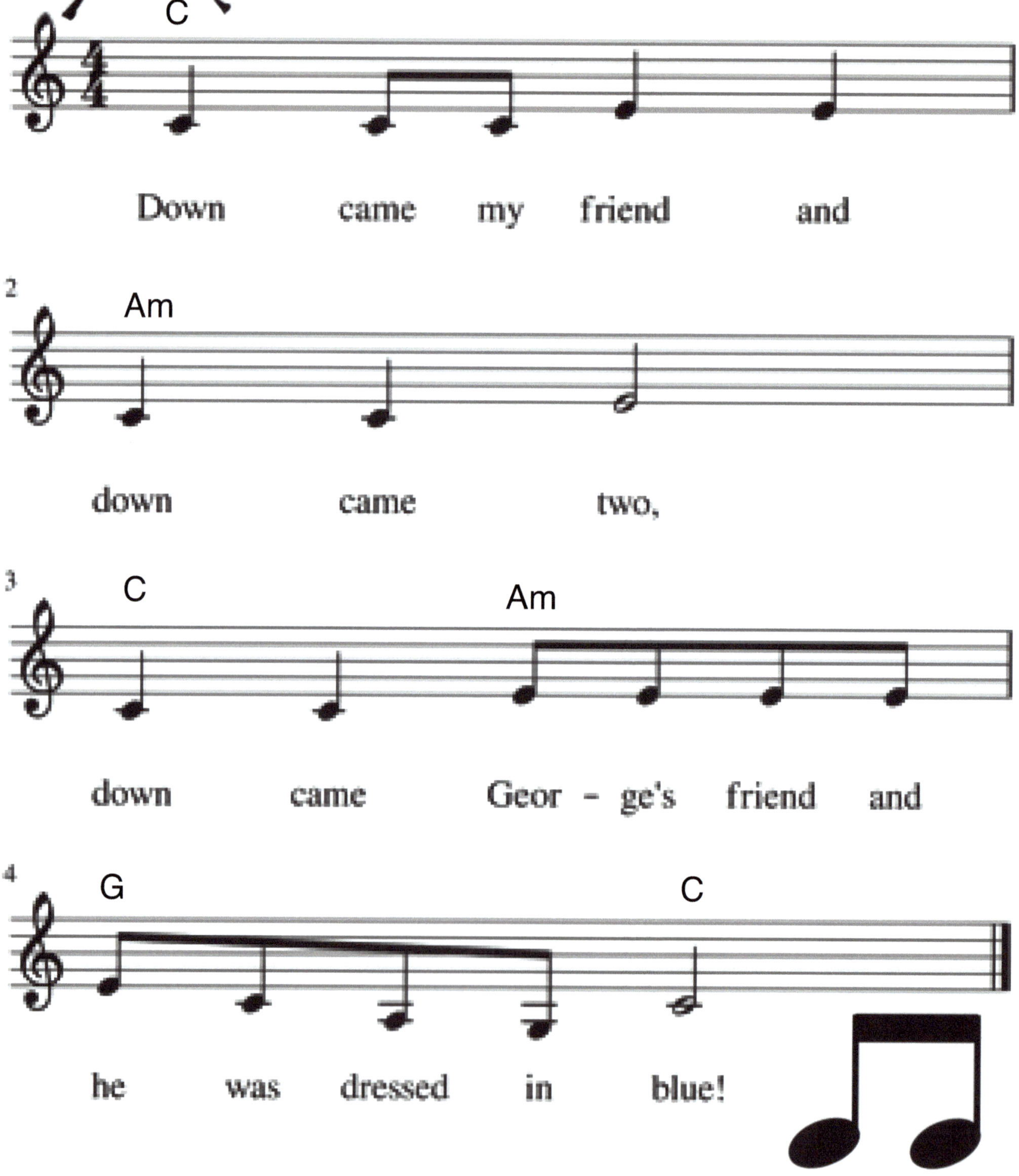
C
Down came my friend and
Am
down came two,
C
Am
down came Geor - ge's friend and
G
C
he was dressed in blue!

Frances Turnbull

There was a Jolly Miller

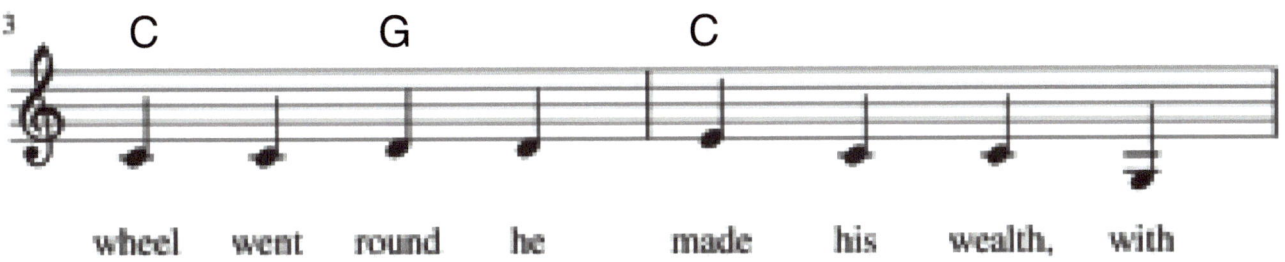

There was a jol-ly mil-ler and he lived by himself, when the

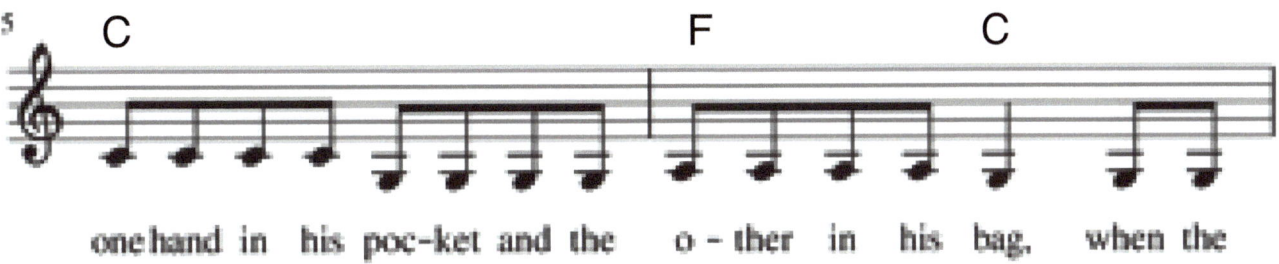

wheel went round he made his wealth, with

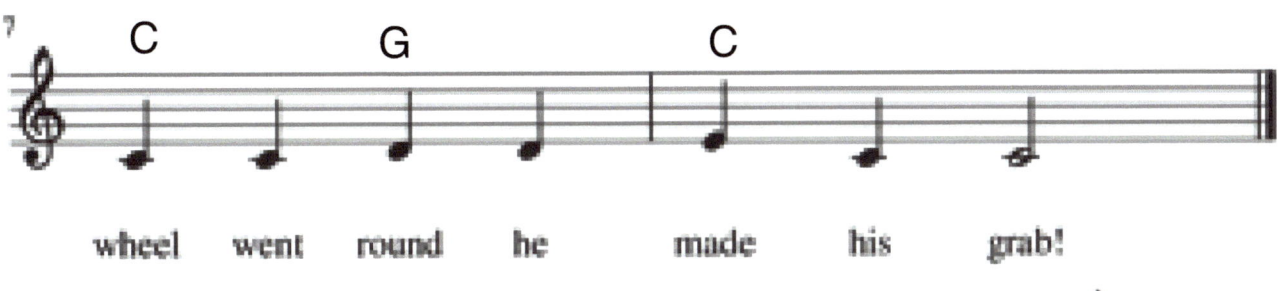

one hand in his poc-ket and the o-ther in his bag, when the

wheel went round he made his grab!

Canoeing

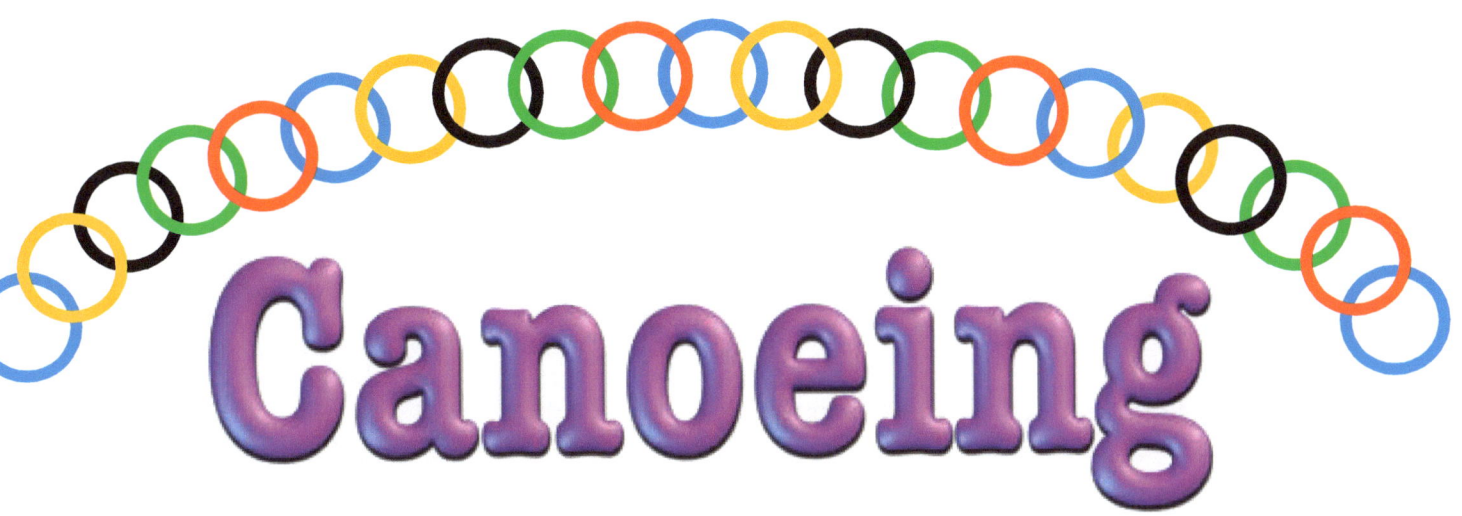

ABOUT KAYAKING
(Olympic sport since 1936)

Kayaking is a type of canoeing that is used in Olympic competition, and athletes can compete in slalom or sprint. Boats can either be canoes for 1 or 2 people, or kayaks for 1 or 2 or 4 people.

Races are usually 500 metres, or 1000 metres, but the International Canoe Federation replaced the men's 500 metre event with 200 metres for both men and women. Women were first allowed to compete in 1948 in the 500 metre kayak sprint and in 1992 in the slalom. Historically, the Soviet Union and Germany are the top canoeing champions.

Musolympics Song Book

GOLD medal 2008

CANOE/KAYAK

Flatwater

TIM BRABANTS

23 January 1977

GOLD medal 2016

CANOE SLALEM

K-1 200 metres

MALLORY FRANKLIN

19 June 1994

GOLD medal

KAYAK (SPRINT)

K-1 200 metres

ED MCKEEVER

27 August 1983

PHOTO CREDIT:
Photo by NHS Employers - https://www.flickr.com/photos/nhse/6353193461/, CC BY 2.0, https://commons.wikimedia.org/w/index.php?curid=51061408

PHOTO CREDIT:
Photo by Ollie Harding from London, UK - Slalom World Championships_15_06_49_30 2, CC BY 2.0, https://commons.wikimedia.org/w/index.php?curid=62824384

PHOTO CREDIT:
Photo by Jim Thurston from London, UK - IMG_0225Uploaded by Kafuffle, CC BY-SA 2.0, https://commons.wikimedia.org/w/index.php?curid=21378688

Tim Brabants MBE was born in Chertsey and is a British sprint canoer. He has been competing since the late 1990's and won the gold medal at the Beijing Olympics 2008 for the Flatwater Canoeing 1000 metre sprint.

He took a year off competing in 2005 to qualify as a doctor and worked as a doctor in Jersey before returning in 2006 to compete in the 2008 Olympics. He is the first Briton to win a gold medal for sprint canoeing. He was given the title MBE (Member of the British Empire) at the 2009 New Year Honours List.

CANOE/KAYAK GOLD
Beijing Olympics, 2008

KAYAK 200M GOLD
London Olympics, 2012

Edward McKeever MBE was born in Bath, Somerset, and is an English kayak athlete. He is the current European and Olympic Champion and former World Champion. He qualified for the final after achieving an Olympic best time of 35.087 seconds.

Ed joined his first canoe club in Bradford-on-Avon when he was 12 years old after a friend introduced him to the sport. He also has a BA Hons in Accounting and Finance, and is studying to be a chartered accountant.

Mallory Franklin was born in Windsor, Berkshire, and is an English triple world champion. She won individual and team events and the overall World Cup title in 2016. In between competing, she studies sports therapy.

When she was 5, Mallory began paddling, and when she was 12, she became the youngest ever British female to enter the Premier Division. Her brother is also a member of the British team in canoe slalom. She trains for 20 hours a week which includes working out and working on the water.

CANOE SLALOM GOLD
Rio Olympics 2016

See Saw

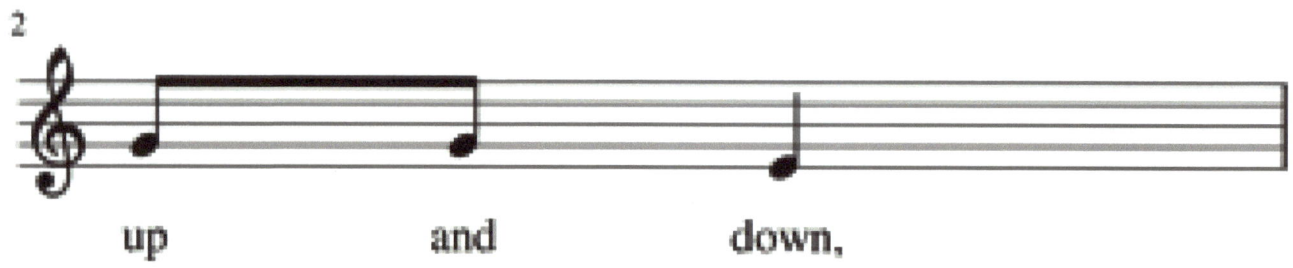

Frances Turnbull

This Way Valerie

This way Valerie, that way Valerie,

this way Valerie, all day long,

Here comes another one, just like the other one,

here comes another one all day long!

Gymnastics

ABOUT GYMNASTICS
(Olympic sport since 1896)

'Gymnos' is Greek for naked, as gymnasts used to wear very little in competitions. The Federation Internationale de Gymnastique was formed in 1881 and is recognised on 5 continents. It represents 3 areas of gymnastics:

- Artistic
- Rhythmic
- Trampoline

ABOUT ARTISTIC

This is one of the best examples of an Olympic event performed on an apparatus and only once ever has anyone achieved a perfect 10 seven times, 14-year-old Nadia Comeneci from Romania in 1976.

BRONZE medal 2008

SIVER medal 2012

GYMNASTICS

Artistic - Pommel horse

LOUIS SMITH

22 April 1989

GOLD medal

GYMNASTICS

Artistic - Floor/Pommel horse

MAX WHITLOCK

13 January 1993

PHOTO CREDIT:
Photo by The Rambling Man and Kim Ratcliffe of Think Equestrian - Own work, CC BY-SA 3.0, https://commons.wikimedia.org/w/index.php?curid=21306943

PHOTO CREDIT:
Photo by los_bandito_anthony from UK - _D703960 Uploaded by Kafuffle, CC BY 2.0, https://commons.wikimedia.org/w/index.php?curid=20712920

Louis Smith is an English artistic gymnast, from Eye near Peterborough.

He is the junior European champion and Commonwealth Games champion for the pommel horse and won a bronze medal at the Beijing Olympics 2008. He is the first Briton to win a medal in individual gymnastics since 1908 and the first black man to win a medal in gymnastics since 1996 (USA).

Louis began gymnastics at the age of four and quickly progressed, particularly on the pommel horse, which became his best event.

GYMNASTICS
BRONZE
Beijing
Olympics, 2008

GYMNASTICS
SILVER
London
Olympics, 2012

Louis Antoine Smith MBE was born in Eye, Cambridgeshire. He is an artistic gymnast, specialising in the pommel horse, and is the first British gymnast to place in the Olympics since 1928. He received a bronze medal in the 2008 Beijing Olympics and a silver in the 2012 London Olympics.

Louis was diagnosed with ADHD when he was a child and was offered a singing scholarship when he was 7 years old. He chose to focus on gymnastics instead, and sacrificed his social life and A-levels to focus on sport.

Max Antony Whitlock MBE was born in Hemel Hempstead, Hertfordshire. He is an artistic gymnast, specialising in the pommel horse and floor exercises, and is the first British gymnast to win gold in the Olympics in artistic gymnastics. He also received a bronze medal in men's artistic all-around competition.

Max started gymnastics when he was 7 with a friend he met at swimming club. When he was 12 he moved to Slovenia with his coach and came back to England to join South Essex Gymnastics Club.

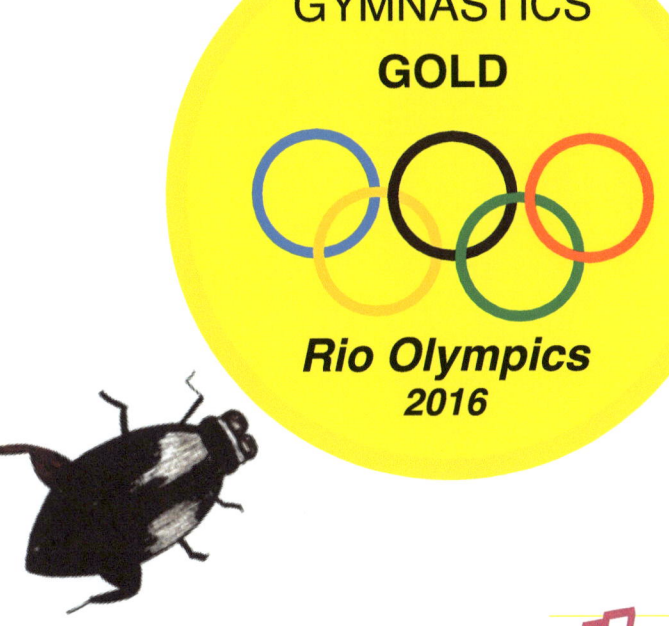

GYMNASTICS
GOLD
Rio Olympics
2016

All around the buttercup

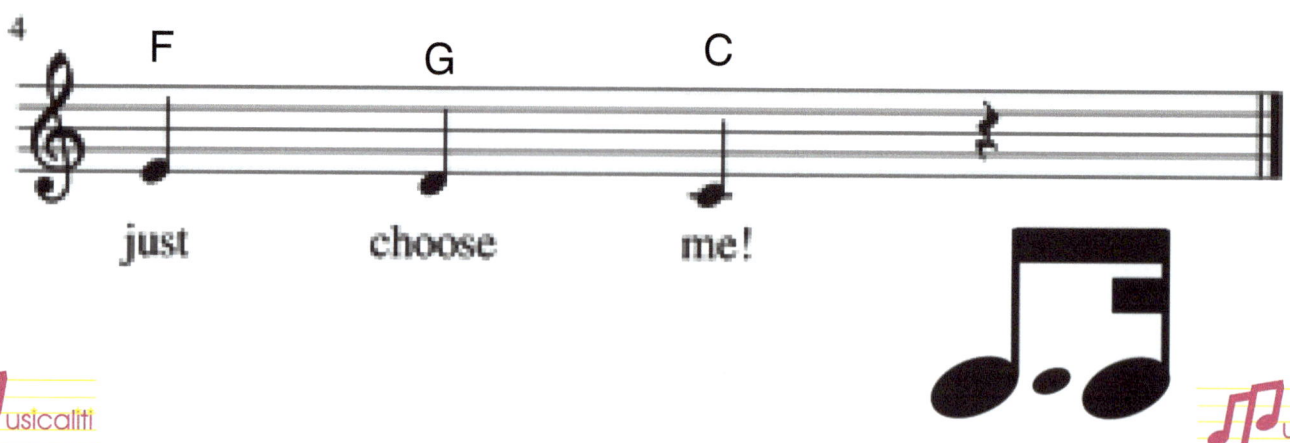

Frances Turnbull

Skip to my Lou

Fly in the but-ter-milk, shoo fly shoo,

fly in the but-ter milk, shoo fly shoo, fly in the but-ter milk, shoo fly shoo,

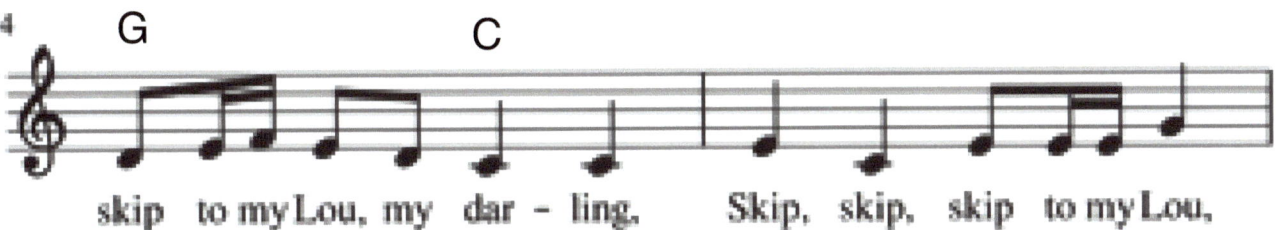
skip to my Lou, my dar-ling. Skip, skip, skip to my Lou,

skip, skip, skip to my Lou, skip, skip, skip to my Lou,

skip to my Lou, my dar-ling.

Musolympics Song Book

Tennis

ABOUT TENNIS
(Olympic sport since 1896-1924 and then from 1988)

There are many tennis competitions, called Grand Slams, and these are run by the International Lawn Tennis Federation, but a lot of players consider an Olympic gold medal to be more important than a Grand Slam.

Depending on the country of the Olympics, play may be on hard courts, clay courts or grass courts, allowing different players an advantage.

While Great Britain has won the most Olympic medals overall, the United States have won the most gold medals for tennis.

Musolympics Song Book

SILVER medal 2012

TENNIS

Mixed doubles

LAURA ROBSON, ANDY MURRAY

21 January 1994   15 May 1997

GOLD medal 2016

TENNIS

Men's Singles

ANDY MURRAY

15 May 1987

PHOTO CREDIT:
By Andy_Murray_and_Laura_Robson_-Wimbledon,_London_2012_Olympics-3Aug2012.jpg: Christopher Johnson from Tokyo, Japanderivative work: Snowmanradio - This file was derived from: Andy Murray and Laura Robson -Wimbledon, London 2012 Olympics-3Aug2012.jpg:, CC BY-SA 2.0, https://commons.wikimedia.org/w/index.php?curid=20559838

PHOTO CREDIT:
By Carine06 from UK - Andy Murray, CC BY-SA 2.0, https://commons.wikimedia.org/w/index.php?

Laura Robson was born in Melbourne, Australia and moved to England when she was 6. Her parents say that she started playing tennis as soon as she could hold a racquet and plays left-handed.

Andy Murray OBE was born in Glasgow, Scotland and was asked to train with Rangers football club when he was 15, but wanted to focus on a tennis career. He has been the British No. 1 player since 2006, won the men's Olympic Gold medal in 2012 and the Wimbledon 2013 championship.

Together, **Laura Robson** and **Andy Murray** received the silver medal for tennis mixed doubles at the London 2012 Olympics.

Sir Andrew Barron Murray OBE was born in Glasgow, Scotland. He has been the British No. 1 player since 2006, and won the men's Olympic Gold medal in 2012 and 2016, and the Wimbledon 2013 championship. He is the only UK tennis player to have won two Olympic singles titles.

Andy started playing tennis when he was 3 and played his first competition when he was 5. When he was 8 he was competing with adults. When he was 15, he was asked to train with Rangers football club 15, but chose to focus on a tennis career.

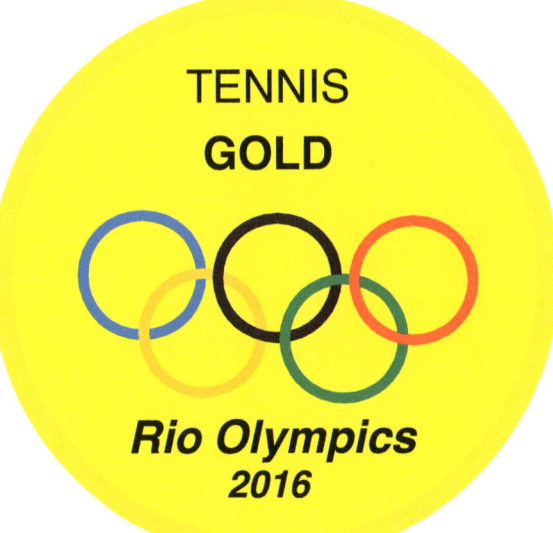

Riding in a buggy

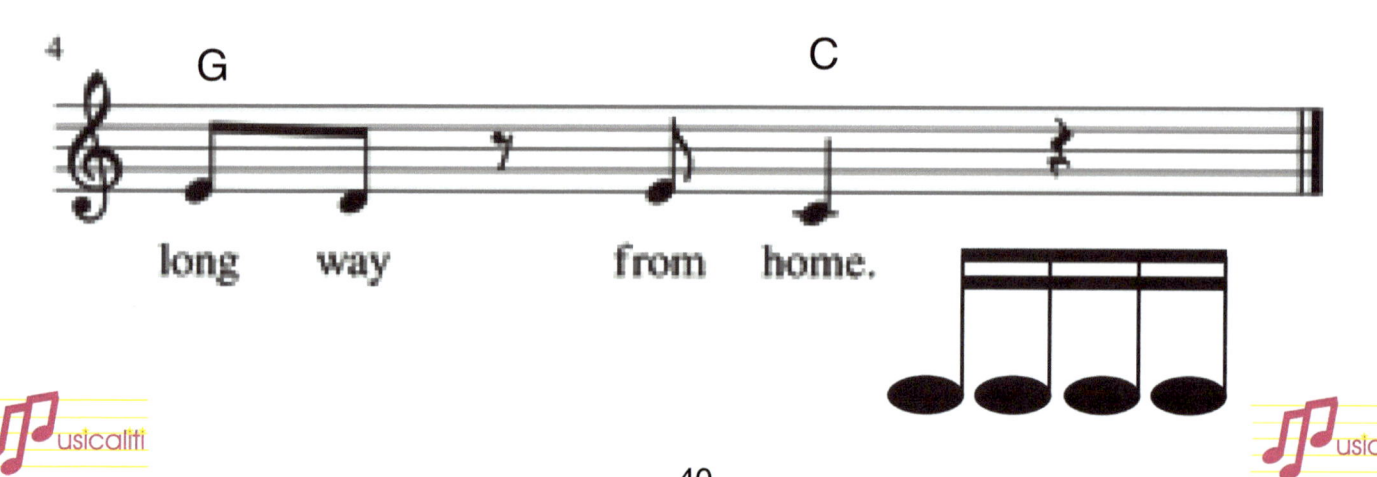

Frances Turnbull

Rover red rover

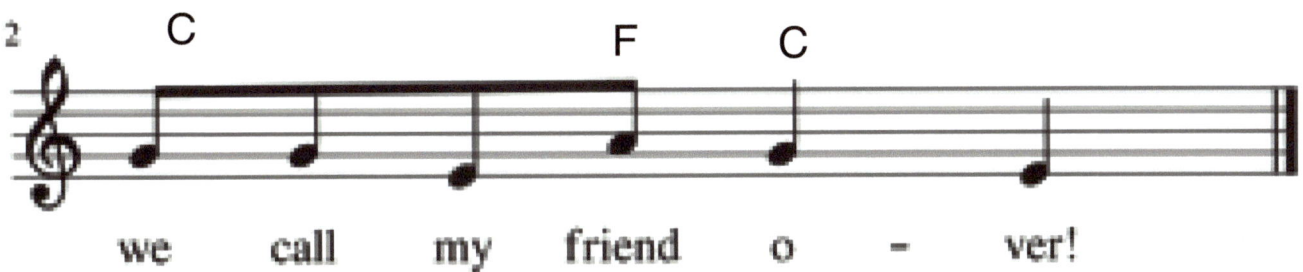

Ro - ver, red ro - ver, we call my friend o - ver!

Musolympics Song Book

Musolympics Song Book

Write your own song

My Song: _____

www.musicaliti.co.uk

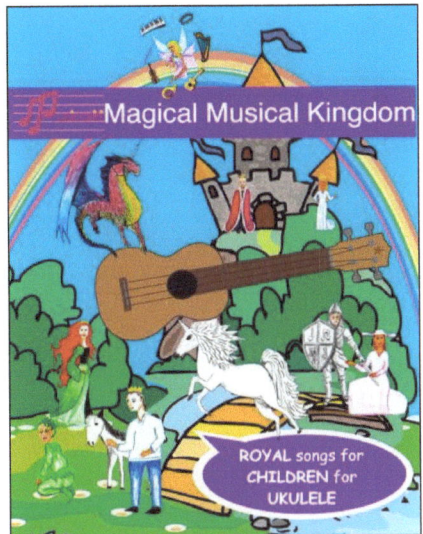

**Magical Musical Kingdom
Ukulele Song Book
ISBN 9781907935770**
Follow the story of King Crotchet and Queen Quaver, and play along on your ukulele!

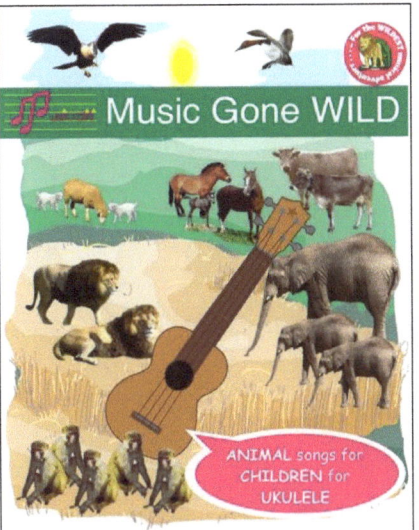

**Magical Musical Kingdom
Ukulele Song Book
ISBN 9781907935770**
Sing about all types of animals, and play along on your ukulele!

**Come and Sing 1
FREE iBook
ISBN 9781907935640**
7 nursery songs are presented in this ibook. Using the Musicaliti skill sequence, develop musical skills using children's songs.

**Magical Musical Kingdom
Nursery Lesson Planner
ISBN 9781907935152**
This nursery planner walks teachers through 10-12 complete music lessons for 2-4 year olds about royalty and magic.

**Yum, Yum, Yum!
Nursery Lesson Planner
ISBN 9781907935206**
This nursery planner walks teachers through 10-12 complete music lessons for 2-4 year olds about food.

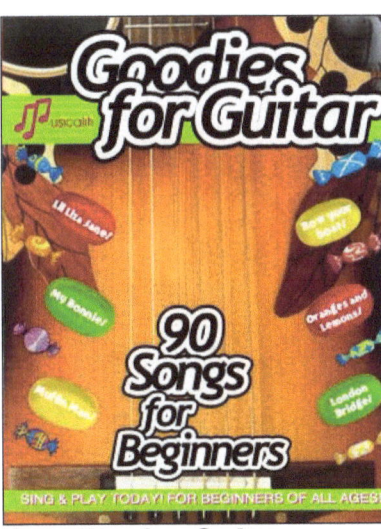

**Goodies for Guitar
Guitar Tutor Book
ISBN 9781907935695**
90 songs for beginners on guitar. Learn about music beats and notes by singing fun songs like Hot Cross Buns and Twinkle Twinkle!

Follow *Musicaliti* on Blogger, FaceBook, LInkedIn, Pinterest, ReverbNation, SoundCloud, Twitter, Wordpress and YouTube

ABOUT THE AUTHOR

Frances has presented early years music sessions in a variety of settings since 2006, after initially training as a secondary mathematics and science teacher. She uses her training in specialist music education techniques (Dalcroze, Orff, Kodály) in her research into the health, educational and developmental benefits of music. Along with writing books, she delivers and develops programs of music sessions for early years, residential and care settings, training courses for providers, and directs a local community choir, the Bolton Warblers.

www.ingramcontent.com/pod-product-compliance
Lightning Source LLC
Chambersburg PA
CBHW041534040426
42446CB00002B/89